Not a Mere Coincidence

Kettly Calixte

Not

a Mere Coincidence

Kettly Calixte

Bibliographic information of the German National Library: The German National Library lists this publication in the German National Bibliography; detailed bibliographic data are available on the Internet via dnb.dnb.de.

Copyright © 2021 Kettly Calixte

Production and publisher:
BoD – Books on Demand, Norderstedt

ISBN: 9783754348352

DEDICATION

I dedicate this book to my deceased little brothers, Marius and Petrus and to my dad. Their lives and non-existence have changed my life and how I live it.

To my loving mom, whose grace and strength is admirable to me.

To my precious son, Noah.

To my wonderful nieces and nephews - Christina, Elijah, Enejah, Kevin, Kyla, Nathalie, P.J., Roberto, Sandra, Stephanie. And my lovely and caring sister, Sandra.

Not A Mere Coincidence

CONTENTS

Not A Mere Coincidence

PREFACE

Have you ever had a friend unexpectedly help you out, resulting in positive changes in your life? Perhaps you've experienced someone calling you out of the blue to cheer you out of your funky mood. Maybe you've discovered a picture, card, or letter tucked inside a book, bringing fond or happy memories that made you smile or laugh out loud, and you momentarily forgot your worries. Have you been on the receiving end of a stranger's kindness, experienced an unexpected victory, averted or survived an accident, or escaped a fatal danger? How about physical healing despite the odds?

I believe some unexpected incidents may transpire to prevent catastrophes in our lives— worse or simply scarier than any mishaps we're experiencing in the moment. People frequently experience such surprises. Yet, in general, we take for granted the "OMG" and "I can't believe my luck" moments. Or we brush them aside as coincidences, or we're unaware of their miraculous nature.

I believe we, human beings, are assisted by an Entity greater and higher than our human will. For me, that force is God, always present and active for our betterment. I also believe that unexpected circumstances serve various purposes: to support, protect, redirect, enhance, and otherwise enrich our lives. Surprises can shift us to a new or better level of thinking and living—a positive change of attitude, a different perspective that encourages and sometimes forces us to grow and change in positive ways.

As I gradually reached spiritual maturity over the years, I began to view situations differently that would have previously thrown me off balance. For instance, losing loved ones taught me the value of family, not taking myself too seriously, and caring more for others. Losing my job propelled me to a better one.

My intention for this book is to challenge you to expand your outlook to view defeats as opportunities, boost your hope in every life circumstance, and recharge you when in doubt. I hope my experiences will also entertain you and help you heal and further grow as an individual.

INTRODUCTION

A vivid, recurring memory from my childhood was a conversation with my then-twenty-something cousin. I was about eight years old when I saw her staring into the sky, her expression pensive. I approached her and asked, "Why do you look like that? What's wrong with you?"

"I have lots of problems," she replied.

"What do you mean?" I asked.

"You're a kid, you wouldn't understand," she dismissed.

Whenever I recall my question, "What do you mean?" I smile and shake my head in amusement. I was completely nescient of life's challenges. Compared to a child of that same age today, I was naïve, being raised in a sort of bubble, protected from the world. For example, it was only on rare occasions that I was allowed to watch television. The amount of time allotted and the type of entertainment was strictly restricted and supervised by an adult. I was always accompanied to and from school by an adult. My friends were my siblings and selective cousins.

Not long after the brief conversation with my cousin, I experienced my first big problem. I learned that my father, barely forty years old, was deteriorating in health, dying from cardiovascular disease.

The loss of my father in my preteens exposed me to grief at a tender age—my first loss in childhood. My father and I were very close, and his passing felt disastrous and unimaginable, marking me. He was a caring father, a good husband, and he was loved and respected by many who knew him.

My mother was a young widow with four young children to raise—my sister, two brothers, and me. But his passing also shaped our lives in positive ways. We were humbled and drawn closer as a family.

The passing of my youngest brother in his late thirties shook me anew. That unimaginable loss brought lots of pain. Watching my mother going through such grief a second time, particularly losing her child, was devastating. Our little brother, whom I referred to as my "lil bro," was gone. I also felt anguish for his two children going through this heartache I knew much too well.

Four years later, my other brother died unexpectedly, holding us in perpetual grief. I was angry, shocked, and devastated. I ached for his three children and shared with them that their dad and two aunties had endured the same feelings when we lost our dad. I reassured them that their love for their dad and memories of him would remain strong forever, and their emotional pain would subside over the years. They were resilient and able to cope with their grief.

My siblings and I were foremost concerned about our mother, as our entire extended family was. We wondered how on earth she'd get through the pain and how the multiple losses would affect her health and will to live.

Somehow, we pulled her through. We all felt comforted by the power of love, family ties, friends, and even the kindnesses of strangers. Gratitude, faith, hope, and prayers gave us divine strength to endure. I'm forever grateful for the divine interventions and people who helped sustain me and our remaining family.

I made peace with impermanence.

No matter how cautious we are in trying to avoid negative experiences by steering clear of the unfamiliar, life does happen, the good and the bad. All individuals carry loads—some folks have bigger burdens or more hurdles than others, but it's all relative. However, how we each choose to deal with our loads is solely our individual responsibilities.

The day I learned about my older brother's death, I was terribly upset with God. I asked, "Why?" and cried, "Not again!" Then I realized this truth: It is what it is, we live through things and go on. We each make personal choices whether to embrace love and everything else life brings, including self-love. My mom was a testament to embracing life through her resilience, strength, and ability to love herself.

As I look back on those past events, I'm thankful to have survived them. I've found wisdom in trials, helping to keep me grounded.

In March 2020, when COVID-19 was declared a global health emergency, two of my primary concerns were staying focused and hoping my loved ones would remain safe.

The pandemic affected the world, all of us, in many ways. The flurry of news from the media, some disastrous, also affected our collective state of mind.

Besides sticking close to my loved ones, praying, exercising, and eating a healthy diet, I found comfort, hope, and encouragement by practicing gratitude. Acknowledging my blessings and remembering how I overcame past crises, sprinkled with unexpected blessings, assured me that my Higher Being (God) is a constant presence in our lives, guiding and protecting us in ways that are beyond our understanding.

As I've experienced, sometimes His blessings are manifested through human actions. Providing help to others and receiving help from others—family, friends, acquaintances, and strangers. Often, we're oblivious to help being provided or don't discern or acknowledge circumstances as opportunities. We fail to draw wisdom, primarily from the bad deeds of others, whether those deeds were intentional or unintentional.

True compassion means not only feeling another's pain, but also being moved to help relieve it.

– Daniel Goleman

Chapter 1

MY LITTLE ANGEL, THAT LITTLE VOICE

Vienna, Austria

It was a Thursday morning during wintertime, and my usual routine had begun. I was bustling about the apartment, preparing breakfast, getting my five-year-old son ready for school and myself for the office. However, I would also be going to court.

I was embroiled in a child custody case with my son's father.

Judging from my demeanor, one would think everything was great, but I was a bit nervous. I was living in a foreign country, Austria, and had not retained a lawyer. Thereby, I'd be defending my argument in the country's language, also foreign to me. Nonetheless, I believed a solution would likely be reached that day, the first meeting and, hopefully, the only meeting.

My brain raced with thoughts. *I need to be there on time, and I need to find a parking space close to the court's building. I hope I understand everything being discussed.* Given that I was a foreigner and my son's father was an Austrian citizen, I could only hope the judge would be impartial. For my child's sake and my sanity, I decided to maintain a positive outlook and be cool as a cucumber in court.

I finished helping my son dress, and we ate breakfast. Then, while he played in his room, I got myself ready. Squatting in the walk-in closet, pondering which shoes to pick, I felt my son's presence behind me. I turned, and he was standing with a gentle smile on his angelic face. He stepped closer to me, stretching out his little arm, and put his right hand on my head. "Don't worry Mom," he said. "Everything will be okay."

I was stunned. His gesture had left me speechless for a few seconds because he was not aware of the adult circumstances leading to that day. As a principle, I didn't talk about adult issues in front of him. Believing he must have sensed my anxiety, I visibly relaxed, smiled, and gave him a hug. "Thank you, my little angel. Yes, there is nothing to worry about at all." Immediately I felt re-energized. *Indeed, everything will go well today.*

Chapter 2

A DRAMATIC DAY

Vienna, Austria

I drove my son to his primary school and during those eight minutes, we made small talk. But on that particular sunny, spring day, my thoughts were heavy. A couple of weeks leading up to the court date, my mind was fully preoccupied with the ongoing child custody battle and some nuisances at work.

Pulling onto the school's narrow one-way street, my stomach tightened at the familiar sight. Double-parked cars lined the short block, and finding a parking space in the area was a rarity.

A car caught my sight, exiting from the curb right in front of the school, and I gratefully slid mine into the vacant spot. Standing in front of me was a child's father at the rear of his car. He hcld a guarded look as his daughter removed her school bag from the trunk and my son exited the front seat to get his school bag from the back seat.

The usual array of parents mingled along the sidewalk, chatting while their children greeted their friends. Anxious about my day, I wondered what was taking my son so long in the back and suddenly heard a commotion and gasps among the parents, and saw a harrowing expression on the man's face, and then heard a mother utter my son's name. As I turned toward the back to see my son, I realized, with horror, I had not shifted the gear into Park and had slipped my foot off the brake pedal. The car was slowly rolling backward as my son was retrieving his school bag.

When he realized the car was moving, he instinctively jumped backward, fortunately onto the sidewalk, as I pressed my foot on the brake, just in time to prevent a potentially fatal danger. I quickly shifted the gear into Park, stepped out of the car, and hugged my little angel. God had rescued him from injury and protected the other children from the trauma that could have been inflicted on them and their parents. A sheer miracle!

Assured that my little boy was uninjured and not too shaken, I released him to find his friends and head into school. When I got back into the car, I said a silent prayer in gratitude, then carefully pulled out to head to work.

By the time I reached my office, I was trembling. I was disappointed in myself for allowing people and circumstances to stress me out and blur my concentration. I sought out a colleague who was like a big sister to me and confided in her. She was older, wiser, spiritually guided, and trustworthy. That was my wake-up call. I needed to practice mindfulness in my personal life and not let outside circumstances distract my attention. She helped me calm down and advised me to recite specific psalms from the Bible. She even printed a couple of verses for me. I was very grateful to have such a compassionate colleague during those weeks and months of stress and the morning's diverted accident. She was also an aid in heightening my spiritual growth.

That evening, after I read a book to my son and tucked him under his blanket, he said quietly, "Mom, you almost killed me." He was right, indeed. I made a pact with him that going forward I would always remain vigilant.

When you see a good person, think of becoming like her/him. When you see someone not so good, reflect on your own weak points.

– Confucius

Chapter 3

THE MUGGERS

New York, USA

New Yorkers party hard. Broadway shows, off-Broadway, off-off-Broadway, dance shows (ballet, contemporary, etc.), nightclubs, jazz bars, cocktail bars, sports bars, rooftop bars, neighborhood parties, backyard and house parties . . .

My friends and I (guys, gals, coupled and single) invariably met up to party on Friday and Saturday nights. Not before midnight, though—nope, that was just not cool.

Prior to hitting nightclubs or whatever was planned for the night, we'd rendezvous either in our homes or at restaurants for dinners. Other times, for convenience, we'd meet up at a subway station nearby to the city and then pile into a taxi to go clubbing. We'd beg the driver to allow more than the law's five maximum passengers, and we'd sit on each other's laps to all squeeze in.

We'd saunter to our elected nightspot, glide through the queuing outdoor crowd, straight to the club's entrance where the bouncer's tense face would relax for a quick minute upon recognizing us. We knew the city, and the city knew us.

Inside a club, more friends would be awaiting us. We'd cha-cha our way to VIP rooms where a second bouncer guarded the entry into an even more exclusive party, sometimes attended by celebrities.

Often, we left one club to go to an after-hours club that opened at three in the morning. To fill our empty tummies and cool our sweating bodies from all the dancing, we'd head to a nearby diner, then finally make our way home. For safety's sake, after a late evening or early dawn, I'd either sleep at a friend's place or take a cab home.

Back then, I lived in Crown Heights, Brooklyn, a blended Jewish and Black community. A car accident had recently occurred in the area involving an African American child accidentally hit by a car driven by a Jewish person. Unfortunately, as retaliation that same week, someone stabbed a young Jewish guy who happened to be spending the summer at his relative's place in Crown Heights. Tension was high, and as a precaution, police were posted on almost every block. So, late one night, feeling safer than usual and thinking I'd save some bucks for brunch the next day, I decided to take the subway home.

The typical one-hour ride stretched into two. The express train had changed to local and paused intermittently throughout the ride, not unusual at that time of night. I had boarded the train at 1:00 a.m., and by the time I exited at my stop, it was almost 3:00 a.m.

An empty station greeted me.

I walked up the flight of stairs facing the dimly lit street where I lived. My apartment building was at the opposite end. Along the street were lots of narrow alleyways dividing single-family homes. The block slanted downhill from my direction, giving me a view of the familiar distance ahead.

When I entered the subway earlier that evening, a policeman was on guard, and I expected to see the same at my home exit. No. Feeling a bit unsafe prompted me to walk fast. For a fit twenty-something-year-old, the average walking distance to my house from the station was seven minutes.

I had walked two blocks when I saw the shadows of two guys in the distance, walking uphill toward me. Intuitively, I slowed my pace and changed my gait. As the distance drew shorter, one of the guys crossed the street, and I knew they were preparing a trap. No matter which direction I could take off running, one of them would be able to get hold of me.

I was scared.

Thinking strategically, I headed into the middle of the street—signalling I was aware of their intentions. I kept thinking, *Oh my God, I am cooked!* I felt foolish having taken the subway at 1:00 a.m. instead of a taxi.

I was in deep trouble, and there was no one around to help—not even a cat or dog stirred the night.

Mobile phones were a luxury back then, the early 90s, so I didn't own one, nor a beeper typical of that era.

I had no place to run and no means of help.

As the two guys got closer, a car suddenly and silently came out of nowhere and stopped next to me, also alarming. The driver asked, "Are you alright, lady?"

Mistrustful in my state of heightened anxiety but searching for an escape, I quickly glanced toward the male voice and stopped walking. I peered inside the car and saw a woman in the passenger seat. Her caring look put me a little more at ease about the male driver.

The lady said, "We noticed those guys tracking you. Would you like for us to drive you to wherever you're going?"

Trembling, I said thank you and agreed, "Yes, they are."

Not feeling completely safe to get into a car with strangers, I countered, "I live just a few meters away. Do you mind driving slowly beside me as I walk and keep talking to me?"

That's how they accompanied me home, rescuing me from an unimaginable fate— whatever it was those crazy guys had in mind.

At the entrance to my building, the couple waited in their car, keeping an eye on me while

I inserted my keys into the two entry doors leading into the brightly lit lobby. Once inside, knees still shaking and heart pounding, I waved goodbye to them, enormously relieved.

Chapter 4

THE APPOINTMENT

Vienna, Austria

Amid an impending divorce, I was in dire need of a different place to live. Despite my tight budget, location was of primary importance to me for my four-year-old son's smooth transition to his new life as a child of divorced parents living in separate households. I wanted a place near his school and still have easy access for him to visit his dad. The frantic search for an apartment started.

I must have visited over twelve apartments before seeing an advertisement for a place that sounded ideal—a sunny two-bedroom within walking distance of our current home and closer to my son's kindergarten and favorite parks. The company I worked for had listed the ad on their website.

I contacted the broker and set an appointment to visit the unit that day, at five in the evening.

Eagerly, I left the office two hours early to allow time to walk to the apartment building and inspect the surrounding neighborhood. Once there, I walked up a multi-level outdoor staircase to the top of the building, where I had a spacious view of the area. Several unit blocks of three- and four-story buildings were nestled together like cottages and surrounded by lots of lush green trees and flowers. I was pleased. I spotted the block I thought was the listed apartment and walked there and waited.

Fifteen minutes past the appointed time, there was still no sign of the realtor. I continued to pace in the chilly air, glad I was warmly dressed. I called the number listed as the realtor's mobile phone, and when he didn't answer, I texted him, to no avail.

Thirty minutes past the scheduled time, I doubted I was at the correct location. Nearby I saw a tenant entering her apartment, so I greeted her and asked, "Is this building number fourteen?"

It was indeed, and I was disappointed the realtor had not shown up. Tardiness was quite unusual for Austrians. Business meetings were handled very professionally, with punctuality as an important factor.

Hungry and disconcerted, I walked home, pondering whether the realtor had perhaps seen me, and decided I wasn't the client he was expecting. There weren't many people in the neighborhood who looked like me, a woman of African American origin.

Memories of an experience six years ago entered my thoughts with renewed force. I had flown from New York to Colorado for a two-day business trip. Given that the Colorado company offices were miles from my hotel, a representative from the company had offered to pick me up.

In the hotel's marble lobby, I stood ready where I could easily be seen, dressed in a high-end, two-piece pantsuit, briefcase in hand. There wasn't much traffic inside, and I noticed a gentleman walking back and forth, clearly looking for someone. *Could that be him?* It was still early, so I waited.

Ten minutes past the scheduled pickup time, I hesitantly approached him and asked, "Are you John Smith?"

With a slight smile of surprise, he extended his hand and said, "Oh! Yes, I am." Dawning on both of us was that he had not expected to see someone brown.

I assumed the same thing had happened with the broker as I waited outside at building fourteen.

The next morning, I called the office in charge of the listing at my employer to vent my disappointment. I received the contact details of the apartment's owner and called her. She offered to show me the apartment the next day. To avoid another possible misidentification, I described myself.

The owner was a slight, elderly lady with a soft voice and open smile. She was very friendly. We exchanged greetings, and I introduced her to my son. To my surprise, she gestured for us to follow her. We walked to a different building within the compound, and I realized I had waited at the wrong place the previous night.

As it turned out, the broker and I had both waited for each other at different locations within the complex. Also, his mobile had lost power; therefore, he couldn't contact me, and naturally left the premises.

The landlady also shared that she had stopped using that real estate company some time ago. "I wasn't happy with their service and listed the unit with another company." (The one I worked for.) "However," she continued, "the broker offered to show the apartment on my behalf for inquiries stemming from the new listing."

As we climbed the stairs to the rental, she added, "He has a prospective tenant in mind for the place, but now that I've met you, I'd rather rent it to you." She smiled at me and then at my son. "I feel a good vibe about you, and I like your son too."

I was elated.

The place was ideal, just as described in the ad: cheerful, bright, and sunny, with a large walk-in closet and two big balconies. One opened alongside the dining room's double doors facing the living room and master bedroom. The other was a winter balcony where we could store toys, play, eat and I could work out on my Cross Trainer machine.

The missed appointment with the broker had worked in my favor. Had I met with him, I wouldn't have gotten the beautiful place he had in mind for someone else. The added bonus was that I saved the broker's fee, equivalent to two month's rent! I used the savings to cover other expenses.

A wrong step had led me to the right place and saved much-needed cash.

The universal law of karma is that of action and reaction,cause and effect, sowing and reaping. In the course of natural righteousness,man, by his thoughts and actions,becomes the arbiter of his destiny.

– Paramahansa Yogananda

There are the waves and there is the wind, seen and unseen forces. Everyone has these same elements in their lives, the seen and unseen, karma and free will.

– Kuna Yin

Chapter 5

You're Fired! Karma

New York, USA

No longer enthralled by the fashion industry I'd worked in for years, I yearned for a change and opted for the publishing industry. I was fascinated by publishing as a teenager, particularly magazines, which, in part, led me into fashion. Given that publishing was the main advertising outlet for the fashion industry, the career switch felt natural.

Although the change entailed a major pay cut and starting at entry-level, I was undeterred. I knew I could move up the ladder quickly since I had solid work experience.

I landed a job as an editorial and marketing assistant for a small publishing company that developed software technology publications and organized conferences for computing sub-disciplines. I was excited to start my new job and learn new skills.

I was assigned a workspace in the corner of what looked like a narrow hallway. Behind me was a doorway to Stanley's office. He was a short, balding, brown man, middle-aged and reserved. Stanley was in charge of managing direct mail and print production. His office was partitioned, creating the space my boss, Kensley, occupied as her office. She was the senior marketing manager overseeing all marketing activities. She was slim and mousey, wore glasses, and had a high-pitched voice and perpetual smirk-like smile, making it difficult for me to ascertain her mood and thoughts, let alone read her expression.

My desk, facing a wall, was filthy and dusty. I spent hours cleaning it as best I could, but the dust eventually gave me an eye allergy. Luckily, with the help of strong eye drops, the symptoms cleared quickly, and I didn't have to miss a day of work.

The office's environment and colleagues were informal and mostly male-dominated, typical for the industry. There were male computer programmers, writers, marketing and sales workers. I greeted everyone I ran into and made small talk with colleagues in the tiny coffee room installed with the printer and fax machine. Through those exchanges, I learned bits about my co-workers' varying assignments and more details about the company's work overall.

My tasks weren't complicated, but I enjoyed the work. My primary responsibilities were to support the editorial department by copy-editing and addressing clients' requests for back issues of magazines. I also helped to support marketing's endeavors to drive awareness and sales of the company's publications. The marketing aspect involved implementing social media, marketing collateral, and publicity efforts.

Two months into the job, I arrived in the office to find three big boxes stacked next to my desk. By the end of the week, the number had doubled. Stanley, who had been working at the company for ten years, had opened one and asked me to open the others. He seemed accustomed to this work and unbothered by the incoming cartons.

The containers held duplicates of the same mail, each addressed to a different name and address. Naturally, I asked, "Why is the mail delivered to our office instead of the folks' mailboxes? Are we in the business of processing them?"

Stanley shrugged and gave little explanation. "These are returned pieces."

Upon seeing Kensley checking the boxes, I seized the opportunity to ask more questions. "Are the envelopes meant for people who are subscribers to our magazines?"

"No," she said, "they're part of a campaign offering a discount to our magazines, and generate leads for further follow-up."

"How do you know who's interested in the offers and where to mail them?"

"We work with other companies that give us a list of names and addresses to mail to," she answered, and I persisted.

"What are we responsible for?"

"The flyers you worked on the other day is an example."

"I see." I thought on that and asked, "What about the returned mail—how often does this happen?"

The color of her smooth pale skin changed to a reddish tone as her eyebrows clenched closer, and her smirk-smile disappeared. "Sorry Kettly," she said flatly, "Stanley can answer your questions when he has time."

Marketing executives spent hours and thousands of dollars designing and writing direct mail packages. But the question of who to mail to has to do with the address list selected—the most critical element. Essentially, the company does everything it can to select the right direct mailing list for a campaign and then refine the list to target individual campaign segments with more precise messaging. For a successful campaign, a company needs good direct mailing list selection and testing. An equally important consideration is that even the best offers can perform poorly if mailed to the wrong target audience. That's exactly what had happened, resulting in the arrival of all the boxes. Kensley had not tested the address lists, which was her main responsibility.

The more questions I asked, the more reticent she had become. Her usual tone was jovial, but that quickly changed when I committed the ultimate sin: inquiring about the returned mail. I had asked questions to simply better understand the business. She became brusque and no longer warm toward me. When I eventually changed positions to another company, I got the fuller picture: Kensley was failing in certain areas of the crucial process, which was naturally causing the company to lose money.

Close to five o'clock one afternoon, the editorial manager approached Kensley and asked if someone on her team could proofread content that afternoon and translate the title to French. The company was considering launching a French magazine, and the editorial manager wanted to present the content to the president as soon as possible.

Kensley asked me if I'd mind undertaking the task, remembering I spoke French. I completed the task right away with enthusiasm while the office was emptying of workers. The editorial manager was thankful for the hurried completion, but Kensley remained mum, making apparent that she didn't like me for some reason unknown to me.

On many occasions, walking through the hallways, I'd pass her as she chatted with someone, and I'd greet them. The other individual would respond, but my boss would ignore me.

One splendid Friday morning, a lady I'd never seen before paid a visit to Kensley. The woman carried a self-assured look that signaled she was not there as an employee but rather like she owned the place and knew the surroundings well.

After about half an hour, she exited Kensley's tiny, windowless office, and less than ten minutes later, she returned, bearing a large box of donuts. She invited me to choose one. Thanking her, I delightedly selected a glazed chocolate donut.

Shortly after, I got a call from Kensley, asking me to come to the conference room. I thought she was going to congratulate me on a job well done since my trial period of employment was near its end.

When I entered the room, sitting next to Kensley, to my surprise, was the same lady. *Why on earth is she here?* They graced me with fake smiles, and I took a seat across from them.

Kensley introduced the woman. "This is Harper Smith, vice president of the company and former wife of our boss, the president of the company."

Unsure what all the show was about, I felt anxious to find out and get this impromptu meeting over. Kensley leaned forward and clasped her hands loosely on the table, and said with uncharacteristic friendliness, "Kettly, I really like you. This is nothing personal." I stiffened inside. Her tone and demeanor were totally different—too friendly—which sounded an alarm in me.

I straightened my back in anticipation of whatever was to come and prayed Kensley would get on with it. *What important message does she intend that warrants the presence of the vice president?*

She proceeded, "We, unfortunately, have to let you go because it's not working out."

What?! Her words felt like a sword into my stomach.

Perplexed and wounded but maintaining my professionalism, I asked, "Could you please elaborate on the reasons you've reached this decision? I was unaware that you weren't satisfied with my work."

She hesitated, "Well, . . . there are a couple of things. For instance, people not receiving faxes they're expecting."

I countered, "I communicate with our clients mainly through email, and on the few occasions I had to send a fax, I always ensured I had a confirmation of receipt."

Kensley shrugged her shoulders and said, "Sorry, there are other things too, which I can't think of right now." I was stunned and appalled. "There's a three-month trial, and the decision has been made to not keep you on." I was speechless and thinking it was useless to persuade her to allow me to stay. The silence in the room was chilling.

Kensley and Harper exchanged a quick glance, and I wondered if the thought between them was of triumph or collusion. The vice president concluded with, "Well, you can take the afternoon off—and next week as well, if you wish, since the month will end soon." My thoughts were spinning in disbelief.

I thanked her, walked numbly to my desk, gathered my things with shaky hands, and left. The meeting had occurred around lunchtime, so the office was otherwise empty.

As I exited the building, I felt like a robot. Blindsided, I couldn't believe what just happened. At the least, I had expected a more complete and concise response to my question. *Why had I been let go?* Searching thoughts of the past weeks and months, I knew I had given myself fully to the work and sought to learn all I could about the company.

When I got home, I cried a bit in anger. Never before was I fired from a job. I called my then-husband to tell him the news. He was compassionate but didn't feel that the loss was worth the heartache. "You can work for a bigger company," he said, "just as I suggested when you were offered that job. You wanted to stick around longer than I thought necessary."

Somewhat mollified, I diligently started looking for another job in the same industry. I contacted a job consulting company and got a few temporary jobs as a proofreader and editor until I could secure full-time work. Within less than three months, I found my dream job!

I was hired as a marketing assistant for one of the world's largest magazine publishers, located in the heart of Manhattan. The company published books and over twenty magazines covering an array of topics—fashion, politics, psychology, travel, food, home décor, and more.

The upscale building was situated just west of Times Square, and some executives had floor-to-ceiling windows giving views overlooking the Hudson River, sixty floors below. The lobby, with marble floors, was protected by well-suited security guards. The elevators, traveling sixty-five floors, were shiny with mirrors. At times, I'd ride the elevators with famous, high-powered celebrities who'd come in for interviews and photographs.

The staff and employees were welcoming and had good attitudes. The environment was upbeat, congenial, and very friendly. I made friends with colleagues who worked for the various magazines housed in different departments on other floors.

My job was on the forty-fifth floor. When first hired, my assigned cubicle was in renovation, and I worked from a corner space. I was handed a catalog to choose whatever furniture I wanted for the cubicle—no budget limit—and anything else I needed to feel comfortable and productive. I splurged and ordered a mahogany-colored wood-textured desk and leather chair. A month later, I moved to the cubicle, the standard type found in New York offices, spacious and brightly lit.

There were many great employee perks. For example, we were allowed to add ten people each to the complimentary subscription list for magazines of their choice. Every month, my tray was piled with magazines I subscribed to for free, and I had access to books for free.

Products used for advertisements and photoshoots were allowed to be purchased cheaply, only $1 to $15 for luxury products from high-end designers. Cashmere socks, silk scarves, calfskin loafers, and more, and the proceeds went to charity.

Another perk was the discounts from business partners we worked with.

Adjacent to the corner I'd first occupied was the office of a sassy, confident, smart, friendly, and well-dressed colleague, Daphne, a manager in the finance department. Through her, I met a lot of colleagues, and she and I became fast friends. She was the one who had informed me early on about the "comp list" her department was in charge of.

There was an air of openness to learn and grow at the company. My boss, Gina, was a wonderful teacher. We worked well together. Everything about my job and the company was opposite from my previous experience.

It was bittersweet when Gina joined a different company, but I was promoted to her post as a marketing promotion manager. It was elating to see my name and title featured on the masthead of the travel magazine I was responsible for.

Life continued to prove that seemingly bad circumstances are often the birth pains that deliver something better.

On my floor was the direct mail department, headed by Gianna. One afternoon, she stopped in to introduce a new temporary employee. My back was facing the entrance of my office, as usual, to better concentrate on my tasks. There were always colleagues walking back and forth in the corridor.

I swiveled my chair around to shake the hand of the person she was introducing and found myself facing none other than my former boss Kinsley. It had been two years since she'd fired me. Surprised but smiling, I said cryptically, "Hi, I think we know each other."

She cocked her head, still smiling, and said, "Really? I don't think so."

"Perhaps, it's my new hairstyle," I offered. I was rocking a short new style.

Gianna's curiosity peaked as she watched our exchange. She was known for gossiping, and I didn't want to say anything that might embarrass Kinsley and feed Gianna's curiosity.

About three days later, I ran into Kinsley in the lady's room, and she hurriedly left, clearly wanting to avoid further conversation with me. That same day, a colleague-friend came by my office and asked, "Have you met the temp? There's something odd about her."

"Yes. I know her from an earlier time. I'll tell you the full story after work."

That evening at a nearby restaurant, I recounted the story to her. Appalled, she said, "Now I know why I felt a bad vibe coming from her. My gut was right."

About a week later, on a very early morning when no one had yet arrived for work, Kensley showed up early and came into my office. "Hi Kettly! My apologies for not remembering you when we were introduced the other day. Now

I do." She continued to babble, "Working at that place was such a bad experience I totally blocked it from my mind."

"I understand." It had been a bad experience for me.

"You must like it here. I saw your name on the masthead of the travel magazine. How long have you been working for them?"

Sidestepping further questions, I answered cheerfully, "They appreciate my work, and they're very nice to work with."

"I hope I can stay. It would be great if the temporary job becomes fixed. "

"You never know," I trailed, feeling sorry for her.

She desperately tried to carve a permanent place for herself in the company, but she wasn't hired beyond the contracted time.

Knowing that disappointments and bad situations can bring much better ones, I hoped Kensley would not ever again do to someone else what she had unjustly done to me. She had fired me simply because I was asking questions to learn more about the industry, which, unknown to me at the time, happened to involve issues with her work performance.

A former colleague from that company had remained in touch with me and told me that Harper was still in love with her ex-husband, the company's president, and she had not liked my friendliness toward him. In truth, I had chatted with him briefly in passing along the hallway and coffee room—as I had with everyone else. Getting fired was a blessing in disguise. Kensley and Harper hadn't defeated me but prompted a promotion for me!

When I'd taken the previous job, I intended to stay at least two years, to learn all I could before moving on to a bigger company. Had they not let me go, I would have most likely missed the opportunity to land one of my most rewarding jobs. It would have gone to someone else who likely would have been promoted to the supervisor's job.

I hoped Kensley had learned a valuable lesson, as we all should in varying circumstances: the importance of not damaging relationships in our personal lives and careers, valuing others for who they are in the moment, sharing knowledge with kindness and respect, and wanting others to succeed.

Chapter 6

THE MINIVAN

New York, USA

It was midsummer. The cloudless sky and warmth created a beautiful day, and I was elated that noon had struck. I rushed from the office, anticipating the sandwich I'd grab at the deli around the corner and enjoying the outdoors. After eating, I walked around the neighborhood to sort my thoughts.

I turned off the busy street and walked aimlessly along a quiet, emptier street. One look at my watch alerted me that my lunch hour was over, so I hastened my steps back toward the office.

Before crossing the narrow one-way street, I stepped from the sidewalk to stand between two parallel-parked cars to peer down the street for any oncoming cars before stepping further into the street.

Suddenly, I felt a jolt against my right arm. *Damn it! Someone just pushed me!* That sort of thing wasn't unusual in a crowded city like New York, and had the street been busy I would have ignored such a transgression and kept walking. However, given that the street was not crowded and I was standing in the narrow space, I felt that the perpetrator could have waited more patiently or taken a different route.

I turned my stern face in the direction of the shove, to rebuke the person, but before I could open my mouth to utter a word, I realized the push hadn't come from a person. The parked, windowless minivan to my right was backing into me!

Instinctively, I jumped onto the sidewalk as the driver continued backward. His van was then consuming the space I had stood in seconds earlier. With one swift motion, he then shifted forward and headed off to his destination, apparently unaware that someone had been standing behind his van.

I could have been crushed to death and left behind, unbeknown to the faultless driver.

What if he had backed up as quickly as he shot away?

That little bump against me was my savior warning.

Standing speechless but safe on the sidewalk, I blinked and pulled in a deep breath, wondrous about the save and what could have happened instead. It was obvious to me that God had protected me. The near-miss prompted me to be more careful crossing streets, irrespective of whether the road appeared trafficless. Also, from then on, I avoided standing behind windowless, parked vehicles to cross streets. I made sure to stand in front of parked vehicles to be easily seen by drivers.

Even chance meetings are the result of karma
Things in life are fated by our previous lives.
That even in the smallest events there's no such
thing as coincidence.

– Haruki Murakami

Chapter 7

THE STRANGER

New York, USA and Paris, France

The subway station near where I'd lived with my mom and siblings was the first and last stop—an advantage of sorts because I got to choose where to sit. During my one-hour morning commute to either the university or work, I'd sometimes read or lightly nap from the two-sitter in the corner of the Brooklyn train bound for Manhattan. Otherwise, I'd observe people getting on board.

Among the usual passengers was a tall, slim, dark girl who boarded five stops after mine. Never in a million years would I have thought I'd cross paths with her in Paris!

Before I dive into that story . . . While attending school in my early twenties, I used to do some modeling gigs. One winter afternoon, I had just left the premise where my agency had sent me to a casting call for a magazine photoshoot. I was leaving the casting place when one of the girls joined me and struck up a conversation. "Hi, I'm Jackie! What did you think about the casting?" Her accent was new to me.

"Alright, but my expectations are not high, from the look of the other models, way taller than me." Walking along the street together, I mentioned I was heading to the subway station to go home. She said she lived not far from the station and would walk there with me.

Along the way, I learned she was from Italy but of Jamaican background and worked as a full-time model. She had recently moved to NY with her American boyfriend. We exchanged phone numbers and became fast friends.

Jackie persistently encouraged me to move to Italy, "where you could definitely get lots of work as a model," she said. "The competition there is less fierce since there are fewer black models in comparison to NY. I travel back and forth to Milan, so whenever you're ready to go to Italy, I'll be there to guide you!" I told her I would give it some thought and she said I could count on her.

My top priority at that time was to complete my university studies. I only had two semesters left.

A couple of months leading to graduation, I had made up my mind about Jackie's proposal. I decided to try my luck in Europe for other opportunities. I called her to share my decision and start making plans, but couldn't reach her. After numerous tries for a few days, to no avail, my disappointment was palpable. I'd never visited Europe and had worked myself into excitement and eagerness, and I was relying on her to navigate the scene in Milano. Whenever I made up my mind to pursue a goal, I didn't relent.

I was at my friend Subi's place one night and brought up the subject. Subi and I had met a year prior in an art course at school. She, her sister, and their photographer cousin said I should follow through with my plan anyway, without Jackie.

"I don't feel confident moving to Italy without a contact there. I've never been there, and I don't speak the language." To my thinking, the move was now out of the question.

"How about Paris? Subi encouraged. "You speak French, don't you? She remembered my minor in school was French literature.

"Not a bad idea!" I said with renewed excitement. Subi got up from the sofa where we were all lounging and walked toward the hallway. Within a minute, she came back, pulling the biggest suitcase I'd ever seen.

With a jovial smile on her beautiful round face, she said, "You can have this suitcase! It's brand new. Come on, you can do it!"

Right then, I was sold on the idea.

The next day, I contacted another friend, Johnny, who had grown up partially in France and knew many people living there. He was also aware of my planned trip to Milan. I updated him with the latest turn of events and my plan to travel to Paris instead. He promptly offered to contact some friends and remembered that he had introduced me to someone whose sister lived in Paris, Jade. He contacted Jade as soon as we hung up. About two hours later, Jade contacted me. She said I would be welcome to stay at her sister's place in Paris.

My plan was set.

With financial support from my brothers, I embarked on a three-month trip to Paris, planning to room with Jade's sister, Sofiane.

I landed in Paris on a Tuesday morning and was quite culturally shocked. The city looked so small and beautiful, and I felt nervous and excited.

The apartment was on the third floor, and my extra-large suitcase barely fit into the smallest elevator I'd ever seen. I loved the apartment and felt at home right away. Situated in a plush neighborhood, it was tastefully decorated and had a little balcony with a view to one of the gardens. Jade's sister welcomed me with opened arms when I arrived and it felt as if I'd always known her.

I was excited to explore the city! I wanted to learn as much as I could about the culture and grow as an individual. But top on my list was seeking an agency to represent me. I was also eager to explore the party scene and make new friends. Both Johnny and Jade had supplied me with a lot of information and contacts.

Come Friday, I asked Sofiane whether she wanted to come along with me to the "it" club Johnny had recommended, Les Bains Douches, a Parisian nightclub in the third arrondissement that at that time was famous. She declined, sharing that the club intimidated her.

I dressed up and ordered a taxi. Solo, I exited the cab in front of the club and walked through the crowd. The doorman, standing atop the crowded front stoop, signaled for me to come in. Inside I discovered a beautiful, glamorous restaurant with chandeliers, a frescoed ceiling, and a double-faced clock. Baffled, I asked the coat checker, "Where's the club?" She pointed to the basement stairway.

The crowd was a cross of clubgoers and creatives, highbrow and low, glamorous and underground, big names and nobodies, all mingling and many dancing on the mosaic floor.

I found a nice spot where I surveyed the electrified atmosphere. I chatted with some people and danced a little bit. Between songs, as the dance floor was emptying, I noticed a girl sitting atop the half wall that separated the bar from the dance floor, opposite where I was standing. Oddly, she looked like the girl I'd often seen on the NY train. Hyperexcited, I walked over to her and said, "Hi, you look awfully familiar. Are you from NY?

"Yes, I am."

"Do you usually take the number four train in the mornings?"

Surprised and smiling, she said, "Wow, yes!"

"I've seen you on the train often." We shared our names and talked until the place was deserted. Her name was Martine, and our friendship started that night.

Like me, Martine was pursuing a modeling career. But unlike me, she had been to Paris many times and visited various parts of Europe. My luck had just changed!

I told her about my plans to visit Italy and London while in France and asked if she could give me any tips. Instead, she offered to accompany me and said she knew all about discounts, sources and the like. No need to use my travel guidebook, after all.

We bought student discount rail passes, I booked a flat for our stay in London, and we embarked on our journey. After a thrilling stay in London for a week, we took the train to Milan, planning to stay four days. I was anxious because we had not pre-booked a place in Milan.

Martine had insisted there was no need. Not my travel style, but I obliged.

Upon arriving, my anxiety materialized when we found no place we could afford to stay. Our budget was modest, and everything was booked, given that we arrived in April, close to Easter.

Four hours into our search, it was 8:00 p.m., and the prospects looked bleaker. By 10:00 p.m., I began to panic. We had to raise the budget from $100 to $150. Still, we found nothing we could afford.

Standing on the sidewalk, contemplating our lack of options, Marine had a brilliant idea. "I can call my acquaintance Fabrizio who lives in Florence, and maybe we could travel there instead." We frantically looked about and found a phone booth next to the rail station. After what seemed like an eternity, he answered the call, and Martine explained our situation. To our delight, he said we could stay at his girlfriend's place. My relief quickly turned to despair as I checked train departures, and I exhaled the caveat: "There's no train to Florence until six in the morning. We need a place to stay tonight!"

We searched the area again, up and down the block, surrounded by all types of accommodations, and we revisited the places we'd checked earlier. Defeated, I turned to my friend and said, "Gurl, we are homeless in Italy! If only you had listened to me before this trip and let me book a place in advance, we wouldn't be in this predicament.

We were both tired, and I was a bit upset.

In desperation, I approached a stopped taxi at the red light and explained to the driver that we were tourists and stranded. He said he had just finished working for the night but could drive us to another part of town to look for a place to sleep. He was young and spoke English very well.

We agreed and climbed wearily into the cab.

We chatted with the cabbie while he drove, and he accompanied us inside each place to inquire about room availability. No luck.

The cabbie then offered to call someone he knew who managed a hotel near the train station. By then, it was close to midnight. There was no vacancy. However, he offered us the doorless room next to the front desk. Fortunately, the opening was draped floor to ceiling. The heavy velvet, red curtain shielded the room from the brightly lit lobby. Inside were two narrow, padded bunks opposite each other.

At last! We had a place to sleep!

Overjoyed and grateful, we thanked the hotel manager and taxi driver. Both men had treated us respectfully and refused our offers to pay. They said they were happy to have been able to help us out.

Our nearly two weeks in Florence were idyllic, and our host, Patrizia, treated us like family. I remained in touch with a few people I spent time with along the journey.

I fell in love with Paris and eventually extended my stay, residing there for two years and traveling to New York every three to six months for visa purposes. I absorbed the rich French culture, everything from its art history and museums to the architecture and food.

I signed with a modeling agency there, got some modeling work, taught English to kids, and worked as a publicist for a small audio-visual firm. The international experience was astonishing, one of the most rewarding experiences of my life, and I'm grateful.

That was my first time living away from home, in a foreign country. The journey was made possible by divine intervention through connectors and facilitators—a network of people, from the person who germinated the idea that I go to Europe to the people who helped me down the line. Most amazing was my encounter with the New York subway rider on another continent, 3,459 miles across the North Atlantic Ocean, and becoming friends.

When I moved back to the States and searched for a job, it was Martine who helped me land one through her sister. Habitually riding a train with a stranger, to her becoming my friend and her helping me on another continent, was not a coincidental encounter. It was a divinely planned adventure of growth and joy by my higher being—God.

Chapter 8

DROWNING

Bali, Indonesia

I love being at the seaside, though I'm not an enthusiastic swimmer. When I was in my early twenties, my then boyfriend would egg me on to hang onto his back while he swam.

We were swimming in his parent's backyard pool in that manner when he playfully flipped onto his back, submerging me. He thought the stunt would trigger me to swim. Not so. Even though he was close by to help me, I was furious with him for scaring me.

A few months after, we were at the beach, in the water. He swam further out, and he asked me to join him. As usual, I stayed near the beach, where I felt comfortable. "Come further," he encouraged and offered his back.

"No way!" I remembered the pool incident and still felt mistrustful of him.

As though he could read my thoughts, he said, "I won't do that anymore. Promise."

I decided to trust him.

I moved through the water, a bit anxious, and straddled his back, wrapping my arms around his neck. He took us further into the deepening blue and flipped me again!

About a year later, we were vacationing at a pristine, serene seaside in Curacao. There was a little island out in the sea within swimming distance. My boyfriend, along with other beachgoers, swam to the island. With envy, I observed their carefree agility and laughter in the clear, calm water. Yet, I couldn't take part in the fun, simply because I couldn't swim.

When he returned and told me how beautiful the island and sea were out there, I realized how much fun and adventure I was missing out on and decided to take swimming lessons.

Within days of returning home to NY, I enrolled in a swim class at my gym. I eventually learned how to float on my back and learned some strokes and breathing techniques that rewarded me with more confidence and comfort in deeper pool water and swimming some distance. Once a month, I'd practice swimming in the pool.

Years later, I was vacationing in Bali with three friends. We'd rented a house that included a rectangular pool, about twenty by forty feet with an average depth of around five feet.

One hot but sublime afternoon, the four of us were cooling off in the pool along the ledges. Bored by the chatter, I quietly swam away, got out of the pool, and walked to the other end. Sitting there and contemplating the water, the pool didn't seem so big, and I considered I could likely swim to the other side. With full confidence, I dove into the water for my solo swim across the length, opposite of where my friends were still loudly chattering.

Like a mermaid with a broken tail, I swam underwater for what felt like a long time before coming up for air. Quickly assessing the remaining distance, I realized I had underestimated the length. I still had a long way to go. I turned back and started swimming to my starting point. When I stopped to get some air, I was startled to find that my feet couldn't touch the bottom to stand without my head submerged. I panicked.

Rolling onto my back, I attempted to float but failed, forcing me to shift back under the water, filling my nose. I treaded underwater, thankful for the swimming classes, and when I reemerged for air, I flagged a hand toward the group, hoping someone of the chatting crew would notice me. They didn't. My trio of friends had their backs to me.

I dove under again and tried to make further headway toward them. Back up for air, I yelled, "Help!" and realized my voice was faint for lack of oxygen and strength and an overload of anxiety. Despite my splashing, no one noticed or heard my plea for help.

As my strength further weakened quickly, my anxiety heightened, and fear of dying in that pool overtook me, sinking my body. In a last-ditch effort for survival, I pushed back up with all my might, twisted my body to face the group, and found that instead, my back was toward theirs.

"Help!" I tried to scream a third time, praying they'd hear me. I was at the point of true exhaustion, made worse by my panicked struggle.

Time had morphed into eternity, and just before my drained body sank beneath the water, I caught a glimpse of my friends turning around and springing forward. They were coming to my rescue.

I felt hands grasping me, shoving me upward in rescue. Taking in air, their arms securing me, I felt a rush of relief wash over my terror.

I was saved, just in time.

Gratitude makes sense of our past, brings peace for today, and creates a vision for tomorrow.

– Melody Beattie

Final Thoughts

As a child, my parents told me we each had a guardian angel watching over us. This knowledge somewhat grounded my confidence toward overcoming adversities and trusting in my well-being. But it wasn't until I surveyed past mishaps-turned-miraculous that I became tightly tethered to my deepening faith in God's presence with me.

The miraculous nature of some of my experiences was not always evident to me. In my early adult years, my responses were surface. *Wow, that was unbelievable! What a coincidence!* I would move on without considering the deeper context. Likewise, I viewed despairing and disappointing instances and events from a shallow perspective. *I'm so unlucky! Why is this happening to me?*

As I gradually grew into spiritual maturity, I realized I had the choice to analyse circumstances and view them in a different, insightful context. I determined to draw wisdom from discernment and found that this practice deepened and strengthened my spirit. My inner awakening moved me to help others simply by sharing my experiences and thoughts.

In tumultuous times, when I feel weary and overburdened, my changed perspective helps to diminish my anxieties, fears, and concerns and recharges me. All the happy memories are now at the forefront, calming me during the storms of life and helping me stay focused on this truth: I am capable, empowered, protected, and provided for—not simply due to maturity but also remaining present in God's ageless presence in and around me.

My parents also taught me to thank God for the day, mornings and evenings. By my teen years, I was doing so innerly. But as an adult, changing my perspective, I came to understand the importance of gratitude.

You may have had life experiences similar to those I've shared, and perhaps you've encountered incredibly challenging and complex situations. Changing my perspective and being grateful in the good and not-so-good times was key to my inner peace, faith, hope, and happiness. How we each choose to view our experiences, process those, and deal with them creates a compounding positive or negative mindset while also considering who we are innately as individuals and our beliefs, values, and desires.

I've heard about and observed that people who experienced the worst of times and survived the harshest challenges are the happiest and most grateful people in the world. They chose to practice positive perspectives in difficult times, embrace unexplainable interventions as divine, and look for silver linings.

What about you? What are your stories you thought were pure coincidences?

I encourage you to write your experiences and reflect on the ones that resulted in positive outcomes. I'm not suggesting you live in the past and dwell on experiences you'd rather keep buried. I'm encouraging you to look at obstacles you've overcome and incidents and situations that took a miraculous turn—a deeper look at the circumstances and moments you savor and appreciate. Your thoughts, mindset, attitudes, and leaning into faith and hope are important. Looking at past, present, and future circumstances and seasons from a deeper and different perspective will be life-changing for the better.

Irrespective of your spiritual beliefs (atheist, agnostic, or a believer in God), distinguish your blessings and acknowledge those. Draw wisdom from your experiences and determine to rid your mind and heart of doubts and anxieties and adopt positivity, trusting in the future.

Be grateful and show gratitude.

Practicing gratefulness is the path to greater inner strength, hope, faith, renewed energy, and reliance to overcome difficulties. Who doesn't want to achieve these?

RECOMMENDED BOOKS

If you or someone you know is coping with the loss of a loved one, the following books helped to clarify for me some issues about death. May you gain peace on your journey.

On Life after Death by Elizabeth Kübler-Ross, M.D.

Proof of Heaven by Eben Alexander, M.D.

Not A Mere Coincidence

ACKNOWLEDGMENTS

Thank you to my dear friend Jill Davis Kone for taking the time to review my book. I'm grateful for her sharp eyes and clever suggestions.

My friend Kettly Dorvilus Delia, thank you for championing my idea to write this book and for making me a part of your family.

Sharon Ehrlich, thank you for your time in reading the chapters.

Thank you to my editor, Jen R. Miller, for her masterful editorial hand.

To all my friends and family who have been so supportive, interested, and involved with my writing, thank you. My relationships with you mean a lot to me. There are too many of you to list, but please be aware that I really appreciate your friendship, love, and support through the years.

Finally, my heartfelt thanks to Lamine Seydi for supporting and comforting me in Austria when I was mourning the loss of my brothers and living far from home (New York, USA). Your presence with me in that difficult time is cherished.

CPSIA information can be obtained
at www.ICGtesting.com
Printed in the USA
BVHW062304011221
622875BV00006B/231

9 783754 348352